Are You Listening?

ARE YOU *LISTENING?*

WEAVING A TAPESTRY
FROM PAIN INTO BEAUTY

ZAYNAB MOHAMMED

Pownal Street Press

CHARLOTTETOWN

www.pownalstreetpress.com

Are You Listening? Weaving a Tapestry From Pain into Beauty

ISBN 978-1-9981292-6-3 (softcover)
ISBN 978-1-9981293-3-1 (e-book)

Development of the play on which this book is based was funded in part by the Canada Council for the Arts, Columbia Kootenay Cultural Alliance & the Columbia Basin Trust.

Pownal Street Press gratefully acknowledges Mi'kma'ki, the ancestral and unceded territory of the Mi'kmaq First Nation on whose land our office is located.

Printed and bound in Canada by Marquis.

1 2 3 4 5 24 25 26 27 28

*To those who loved me through thick and thin,
and to those who let me love them through
turbulence and triumph.*

Contents

Contents

MAP OF MY HEART

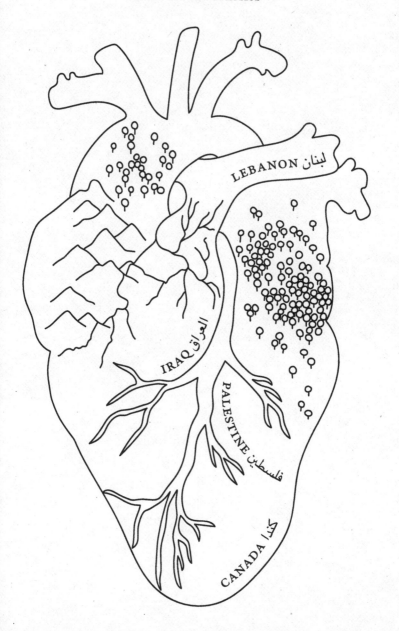

Intro

NIGHT PRAYER. SALAT EL-LAIL. It is said to be the best time for intimate contemplation with God in the Muslim faith. My mother had converted to Islam a few years prior to my birth and loved her newfound religion. When I was growing as a fetus in her womb, she would wake up in the middle of every night to pray.

As the hour of my birth approached, she practised one last night prayer just as dawn was peeking over the horizon.

Hardship is inevitable. She could only protect me to a certain degree, for life is bound to leave its marks, scars of victory and defeat, on the brave souls who walk through it.

والدتي تحبني، أنا كنز لها. لقد حمتني صلواتها طوال حياتي بطرق تبدو وكأنها معجزات.

My mother loves me. I am a treasure to her. Her prayers have carried me throughout my life in ways that look and sound like miracles.

9/11

I WAS BORN A BROWN-SKINNED MUSLIM GIRL in
British Columbia, Canada. My parents immigrated to
Canada separately in the 1970s and 80s. My dad left Iraq as
a university student, during the Saddam Hussein regime in
his early 20s. Mom left Lebanon as a young adult during the
civil war, just as Israel was invading her country. They met in
Quebec through friends, got married and moved out West.

My brother and I were born in Western Canada.

After six years of marriage, our parents split up. I was
three at the time.

We were raised by our mother during school days and
went to our father's house on the weekends. It was what
we knew. It was our life. And we lived it, as children do, innocent in our imagination and curiosity. We were far from
knowing the responsibility and harsh world we would grow
up and become part of.

At some point my father found a new wife and created a

new family. His wedding was just two days before the Twin Towers attack in New York City. On that day, I turned 11.

Over a few short seasons, I remember life dramatically changing. Someone told me that the number of the day of the month you're born on is the age when a big traumatic event happens and changes you.

I was born on September 11th, and on my 11th birthday the Twin Towers were struck. I was in grade 6 at a middle school, with a teacher I never grew fond of. In this class, with this teacher, in this 11th year of my life, I learned that Palestine didn't exist anymore, at least not on the map, even though I knew my grandmother was born in Haifa, Palestine, in 1936. She fled in 1948 with her family during the Nakba (the catastrophe) along with 750,000 other Palestinians who were forcibly removed, ethnically cleansed from their lands by the Zionist regime.

So on September 11th, 2001, the discourse in our home, in my family, was different from what we heard at school.

You see, my homeland. The countries my parents grew up in have been, still are, continue to be, graveyards made by the US army. By the French army. By the British army. And by the Israeli army.

Only recently, after much discourse while speaking with a friend, did I finally realize how glorified war is in our society and culture.

ZAYNAB MOHAMMED

من يستطيع تصور عالم بلا حرب؟

Who can envision a world without war?

It seems unfathomable to most people. People believe that to get what we want, we must use force. It's how our leaders reflect their unwavering missions through war and destruction. But there have got to be other ways that don't involve killing sprees or power over politics. What would the world look like if we replaced our triangular hierarchy with a circle? A system of real equality. Is this really so hard to imagine and implement? A redistribution of power is called for!

ARE YOU LISTENING?

So on September 11th, 2001, as I blew out my candles and made a wish, I wanted my classmates to know about Palestine's brutal occupation. I wanted them to know that we—Iraqi, Lebanese and Palestinians—have suffered thousands of 9/11s. I wished for the death toll in my homelands to be a life stopper for the people I shared a classroom with. I wished for Arabs to be more than statistics and headlines in the news. I wished we weren't so othered by this normalized white-centric society.

To this day, I wish for people to know about Palestine and the horrors Palestinians have had to endure for the past century and counting. My mother says if you admit that Occupied Palestine (Israel) is a nation, you abolish Palestine. Palestinians have no nation. It's been taken from them. They've become refugees with no status of statehood in their homelands or in neighbouring countries. Some have been granted passports of other nations. Many have become Israeli Palestinians living in the Occupied Territories.

But no one stopped to tell me, to tell all my peers, the story of Palestine. About how there are eight-metre-high concrete walls and barbed wire fences that surround the Gaza Strip and half of the West Bank, separating the Israelis from the Palestinians. Checkpoints every few kilometres. It wasn't mentioned that Palestinians have no rights and live in an apartheid state, or that Gaza is the biggest concentration camp or open-air prison in the history of time. This crime not only continues, but escalates to this day. Because they are born in a war zone, Palestinians are under military watch. Born as an enemy.

I often wondered to myself, how is this justified? Why is some blood worth more than other blood? People are paid to be soldiers, paid to do the dirty work of politicians. People are trained to kill. This is normal in our society. The violence in this world is like a virus; it infects our minds and steals our hearts.

So on September 11th, as I blew out my candles, I wasn't distressed like my classmates or my teacher. On September 11th, when I turned 11, a year after I got my period, two days after my dad got remarried—on that day, it hit me. Me and my family live in a totally different reality than the society I grew up in. This day changed everything, and our lives would never to be the same.

It was all over the news: Muslims were to blame for this tragedy. *El-Musilmeen.*

MUSLIMS.

US.

We were made out to be the enemy. Because that's how history works. Arabs became scapegoats for North Americans and the next common enemy was born.

My 11th birthday was officially the end of my childhood.

It was the end of innocence and sweetness in our family. My 11th birthday is when my family's destiny was written by the same hands that made us immigrants fleeing war-torn countries. On my 11th birthday, I said goodbye to Barbies and hello to becoming *numb*. I said goodbye to playfulness and hello to attention and popularity—but the wrong kind. On my 11th birthday I said goodbye to being just another person in society and hello to being people's enemy. On my 11th birthday, I said goodbye to being happy and started to be angry.

Days after, my mother lost her job because she wore a hijab—a headscarf—as part of her religious practice, and she couldn't be the face of her office anymore. Instead of suing or fighting for her job, she turned the other cheek. On our outings, we were often stared at more than before the 9/11 attack. I began to carry deep shame towards my heritage. This shame, coupled with teenage-hood and its overflowing well of hormones, was the perfect recipe for rebellion and dissociation from the dignity and culture I was raised with.

I did everything I could to fit in, to hide my Arab heritage, and to not be seen with my mom. I discarded the nuggets of tradition that could protect my angry heart. If there had been other Arabs around, which there weren't in the city we lived in, perhaps I would've felt solidarity with them and moved closer to my identity. This pushing away of my identity spun me into years of disillusionment. School was a downhill spiral. Drugs and alcohol became my friends. I got into unhealthy situations that thankfully never swallowed me whole.

A year after my 11th birthday my big brother was arrested for playing with firecrackers. He and his teenage friends would take apart small fireworks and reassemble them so that they would make bigger and louder booms. This was simple entertainment for them, and they only did it for fun. They never harmed anyone.

My brother hung out in a group with four other teens, and they all played with these firecrackers. They would buy them from pop-up shops on the side of the road on holidays like Canada Day or Halloween. It is a tradition in North America. These kids simply wanted to be inventive. My brother, in those years, also took apart computers and reassembled them. He liked to carve wood, and Mom assigned him all the home fix-it jobs.

When the authorities caught wind of these teens, these kids, playing with fireworks, they focused on my brother. The other four teens didn't get harassed or investigated. Only my brother: the brown-skinned Muslim boy.

The cops showed up to our house, and my mom, who didn't know her rights, let them in. They searched our home. We had to leave. The SWAT team came in.

My brother, who was 17 at the time, spent three days in prison. My parents were beside themselves in disbelief, shock, and prayer. Shortly after his release, we got evicted from our home. We were told that we were a danger to our neighbours.

Thankfully, my brother was a minor, and he didn't get a criminal record. He went to court and faced some hefty penalties, like a curfew and no internet. It didn't make sense. This same court holds laws that allow our countries to be blown up.

Have "Western" countries ever been held accountable for the massive destruction they've either participated in or been part of funding in the countries my family is from? Yet my brother is put in his place, while these countries are not, hence they continue to fuel and fund war on our lands. The courts cannot stop them. It seems no one can.

Getting kicked out of our home was the last straw for my mom. She was done with Canada. Done with racism. Done with living a lie dressed as another chance to live a decent life in this country.

So, she decided to write a new story off this land that my brother and I were born on. My brother stayed in Canada and moved in with my dad and his new family for his last year of high school. And I moved to Beirut, Lebanon, with my mom.

Beirut is a hard story to tell. It's the greatest love story of my life. When I went from Canada to Lebanon, I met my roots, my language, and my people; it altered every ounce of my existence. It was a homecoming full of rage, anger, and frustration, a novel in itself, really. Beirut stole my heart by breaking it repeatedly. Love and hate filled every moment.

How do I describe a country, once called the "Jewel of the East," that is now beautiful chaos and is full of corruption? How can I orchestrate words to relate this broken heart of mine when I look in the eyes of my motherland? How do I transcribe belonging without my mother tongue?

Home Is . . .

Where people walk around carrying the weight of a dark
history in silence.
Where war has come and gone, and can come back again
in any given moment.
A place that hasn't had a break long enough for the grief of
loss to begin to heal.
A country that knows of its beauty, yet still sings of all that
has been lost.
Where lines are drawn between sects and religions and
neighbourhoods.
Where there seems to be no end to suffering.

Lebanon was a three-year tale for me. High schools and
friends and cigarettes.
Makram became my best friend and thankfully still is.
Dreaming, only the ones who make it out alive are allowed
to do such a thing.

The ones left behind are hostage to corruption.
It's a game of luck and privilege in my homeland, too.

There isn't an easy way out.
I was always referred to as an outsider.
People thought being from outside was better than being
from inside, and in many ways, it is.
I get to have freedom of movement.
This has come at a high price, a life filled with longing to
belong to my people from afar.

Orchards

البساتين

لا أريد أن أغضب
لا أريد أن أضيف إلى آلآم العالم عندما أتحدث

I don't want to be angry
I don't want to add to the pain of the world when I speak

I want my words to be like seeds that blossom
into orchards of fruit trees
That feed people sweetness for generations to come
I want my words to bloom like flowers
To be pollinated by bees
To meet your ears

So that the continuum of magic spreads
So that our hearts are filled with sights of how precious
Is each breath that gives us
Another moment to appreciate life

Because the pain is real
And when I'm not looking, I remember my roots
The women before me
And how being a woman was never a good thing

Was never celebrated, praised or respected
At least if it was, I wasn't taught or shown that the blood
That rushes from my body every month
Is the most precious part of my being

That it carries the seed of life in it
That I am like that fruit tree

I am like every blossoming flower
Though not pollinated

I still bloom and shine
Because that's who I am
A life giver

I am a woman, with a womb, with a story
Searching to relieve the pain that I carry

Is being a woman synonymous with pain?

منذ ولادتي قيل لي
أن أبقى صغيرة
أن أكون صامتة
أن أغطي بشرتي
أن أخفي مشاعري
أن لا أكون من أنا
ولكن ماذا يظنون أنه علي أن أكون

Since birth, I was told
to stay small
to be quiet
to cover my skin
to hide my emotions
To not be who I am
but who they think
I should be

You see, I have set myself free
And now I am setting my story free
Because orchards are in droughts

In my homeland, on my family's orchard

During the civil war and the Israeli invasion
The fruit trees that my grandfather planted
were cut down for firewood
So when I go to visit
The land is bare, covered in thorns and weeds, overgrown
with grass and layered with bullet shells

In 2017 on a visit to Lebanon
I spent six months in our village
During that time an elder came back to her home after
decades of reckoning
Forty years prior, during the civil war, she witnessed her
family members being murdered, in her home, in our village
She escaped the blood bath
She became a nun, and
dedicated her life to serving children

When she was ready to face the scene of the crime, I was there
She knew my mom from over 40 years ago

She knew my whole family

She gave me a tour of her home, shared her story with me
I sat with her on her deck

You see, her story is one in a million, one in millions
Stories like this continue to this day
Because . . .

Orchards in drought are being cut down for firewood

I will not end my story as ashes to fertilize land
I will take these ashes and revive them like an alchemist
I will turn these ashes into words
I will blow these words into intrinsic landscapes

I will make them ecosystems
I will plant orchards
Because I don't want to be angry
What I add to this world
In this blip of a moment while I'm living
I want it to be beautiful
I want my words to create orchards

Of sweet fruit to be enjoyed
And digested into life juice
The sustenance we need to move through
Fields of orchards in droughts being cut down for
firewood

I want to be part of planting a legacy that surpasses war
and human greed

That goes beyond you and me and becomes a gateway
For what we can't even imagine yet
A world where beauty is so intoxicating we become
drunk poets
Piercing through the veil of audacity and transforming
our pain

Into beauty, into magic, into possibility
I want my words to set me free

To let me see
That I am beautiful

Not despite the pain, but because of it
Because I never let it steal my heart

Although it hurts to pass through the eye of a needle
I did it, I learned and continue to learn how to look at pain,

how to feel grief, how to thank suffering

And how to turn crisis into opportunity with the ink I
write my poetry with

Dear Four-Year-Old Self

عزيزتي ذات الأربع سنوات

حبيبتي يا أغلى حبيبة
أمامك طرق كثيرة
آه سوف تتخذين الكثير من الخطوات
طفلتي العزيزة، نفسي البالغة من العمر أربع سنوات

Beloved oh dearest beloved
Many roads lie before you
Oh so many steps you will take
Dear child, my four-year-old self

You are pure, like an owl
Soft like its feathers
Present with your eyes
Staring out to the sky

Innocent and brave
You have come to be changed
To evolve and transpire
To erupt and prosper

It is no small deed;
You have summoned what you need
You have orchestrated as a seed
Sprout slowly into your breed

Dear darling Zanouba
The pages turn and leave a mark
It will hurt—it will shatter
It will be incomprehensible

For you are four
You do not know
You do not see
The pain behind the screen

They mean well
Your mama and baba
Limited and fractured
Displaced from their lands

It is hard to be displaced
To be far from family
Far from culture and friends
But people can start again

They did with you and with your brother too
They gave it what they had

Your will is strong
Your sight is clear
Tread softly
Do not fear

You may not know
The price to pay
It is an exchange
You will have to give
Your innocence

This price is steep
It comes from your dreams
It is the rocking of your ship

You need to bend
To break
To shape
To forget who you are

It is a journey
No ending point
You must walk every step

And look ahead
Look into
The threads of the making
The stories we weave
They come and tease
Though joy is far from waking

Lebanon, My Heart

لبنان قلبي

إحتفلت بعيد ميلادي الرابع عشر في بيروت لبنان، مقيمة
جديدة في البلاد. سيكون عيد ميلادي الأول بدون أخي الأكبر.

*I celebrated my 14th birthday in Beirut, Lebanon, as a
new resident of the country. It would be my first birthday
without my big brother.*

WE HAD SPENT NEARLY EVERY DAY of our lives together before me and my mom moved to Lebanon. Me and my brother's nervous systems regulated one another's. We were each other's lifeline; and now we lived more than 10,000 kilometres apart.

He's told me in recent years how shocked his nervous system was without me, too. He short-circuited and stopped dialogue with me after I left Canada with my mom. We had never had a long-distance relationship. We didn't know how. He is the type of person who doesn't text or call back regularly, let alone send an email to let you know he's thinking about you. The distance between us evaporated our relationship.

For me, I had my other lifeline, my mom. For him, he got my dad and his wife. Although he got to stay in Canada, he was uprooted from what he knew his whole life. One of the reasons my mom didn't bring him with us was because one of his penalties for his incident with being arrested was that he could not leave the country for one year.

Lebanon was a major culture shock. I was so mad at my mom for bringing me there. Even though hearing and speaking my mother tongue was soothing, I was furious to have left my brother and my dad and all my friends.

Going to school helped. Making new friends helped. Strengthening my Arabic helped.

Slowly my relationship with my mom improved. We were bonding in new ways. She would share personal stories of her lived experiences as a teenager growing up in Lebanon during the civil war. This helped. I got to see a side of my mother that was hidden up until our time living on our homeland.

Lebanon's history is rife with politics. Within my first year there, the ex-prime minister of the country was assassinated by a huge suicide bombing near Beirut's seafront. Twenty-one other people were also killed in this attack. The country had been at rest for some time up until this moment. But from then on, unrest followed.

About a year later, when I was 15, after completing grade 10, more unrest met the shorelines of Lebanon.

On July 11th, 2006, I could not sleep. I had a handful of photos I had recently gotten developed and had the urge to create a collage. Portraits of my friends and I at school reflected the sweet memories of my first couple years in Lebanon. I worked on this collage through the darkest hours of the night. Before dawn, I took a sleeping pill and went to bed.

A few hours later, my cell phone vibrated on my bedside table and woke me up. It was Ruba, my best friend, calling me. "Hello?" I said, picking up the phone. "Zaynab, are you home?" she asked. "Yes," I answered. I wondered why she had called my cell phone rather than the landline—calling a cell phone is three times as expensive as calling a landline in Lebanon.

"Zaynab, they bombed the runways! Did you hear it? Are you ok? You need to leave your house right away! A war has just started."

This was the beginning of the 2006 war.

Still weary from my all-nighter and the lingering effects of my sleeping pill, I told her that I would talk to my mom and figure something out. We both said, "I love you! Stay in touch. And be safe out there," before ending the phone call.

My mom confirmed the news. I was horrified, whereas she was not fazed whatsoever by this abrupt change of weather.

The war shaped me into the person I am today. For better and for worse.

DAY 1

I go to stay at my Téta's (grandmother's) house in a safer part of the city. Mom stays home. My aunty and two cousins show up at my Téta's and we all stay there together.

Night 1: Every time my eyelids grow heavy, a bomb goes off. Explosion after explosion for hours on end. My Téta's home, though relatively distant from the bombings, trembles with every attack, and leaves our spirits alert and awake.

DAY 3

I go home. I need somewhere else to stay. The politics behind this warfare doesn't register in my 15-year-old mind. My aunt says I should leave Téta's house because of an innocent remark I make in regards to the unfolding devastation before us.

Night 3: After passing multiple blown-up bridges and demolished neighbourhoods that were filled with life just days prior, I arrive at home. Unsettled, nervous, and fearful of the horrors, I begin to wish I could leave as soon as I'm home. The streets are deserted. Our neighbourhood is nearly vacant. We live in the southern suburbs, a dangerous part of the city in regards to this war.

DAY 4

Our propane cylinder runs out of propane. Thankfully, when I go to get it filled, the man who sells propane is still there. I find him packing up and closing shop. He fills our tank and I carry it home and up the five flights of stairs to our apartment.

Night 4: At dusk, an Israeli MK aircraft hovers metres above the buildings, scanning for heat, gathering data for their war strategy. This low-flying aircraft feels like an earthquake for us inhabitants of these six-story concrete buildings. We've cracked open all our windows at home so that the glass doesn't shatter from the effect of the MKs or nearby explosions. Our most valued personal belongings sit at the front door in one small suitcase and one large purse, in case we need to make a run for it. My mom and I stay in the same room. We sleep in the same bed. Once the MKs move past our neighbourhood, the air is thick with silence. A rare occurrence in Lebanon. No cars honking. No night prayer on the megaphones. No one is selling fruit from carts on the streets.

This marks the transition from a peaceful day to a shattering night. About an hour after the MKs vanish, the bombs start dropping. They come in sets. Like waves on the ocean's shore. We try to make out the proximity between the explosions and us.

The bombs rattle our home. Rattle our being. We tell jokes and relish in memories. It is somehow a hilarious, un-believable moment in our lives that calls for releasing all the stress caused by such madness and absurdity.

DAY 6

Natalie, one of my dear friends, agrees to my request to come stay with her in her home in Alley, a mountain city 15 kilometres north of Beirut. Natalie was born in the US to Lebanese parents. She moved to Lebanon one year after me, with her sister, wanting to connect with her roots.

Night 6: Natalie's boyfriend and his cousin pick us up. We drive to one of our favourite viewpoints overlooking Beirut. On our way, we pick up a bottle of vodka, orange juice, Redbull, potato chips, roasted salted nuts, and a couple of packs of cigarettes. The price of these goods, because of the war, is three times more than what it was a few days ago. We don't care about the cost. We're invested in the moment and the final memories we know lie ahead.

We sit close to one another on a rocky cliff, across the way from an old and active minefield that was planted by the Israelis during their occupation of Lebanon in the 1980s. We mix our drinks, graze on snacks, and talk for hours about all the good times we have shared. Natalie and I plan to get evacuated by the US and Canadian embassies. This is likely the last time we will all be together.

We spend hours at this viewpoint, crying, laughing, and speaking about all our adventures over the years. None of us hold back any emotions, thoughts, or sentiments. All the while, we are witness to bombs being dropped on our beloved city. We see big orange balls fall from the sky, which in reality are bombs being dropped from an Israeli aircraft. This is followed by a bright light that comes from the land below us in the not so far distance. Every orange ball, every bomb dropped, shakes the earth we sit on. This rattles our guts and breaks our hearts.

We watch the show in the sky for hours. Life, as we know it, is shattered with every building coming down. Our emotions override the effects of the alcohol we drink. Watching Beirut get bombed provokes a feeling unlike drunkenness. This feeling is hard to describe. It is as if time doesn't exist and we are in a dream, hoping that we will wake up from this nightmare.

DAY 9

I get an email regarding my registration with the Canadian Embassy to be evacuated. They say to come, with one suitcase, my passport, and a big patient heart to a specific stadium at the Port of Beirut. My mom's friend drives us. Upon arrival, the folks at the door let us know that they're at capacity and to come back the next day at 3 PM.

We drive back home, through the deserted streets, just as the sun begins to set. We avoid highways and go through smaller side roads to get to our neighbourhood, now nearly devoid of humans. A couple blocks before we arrive at home, what sounds like nearby gunshots to me makes our driver, my mom's friend, accelerate until we reach the entrance to our building.

Night 9: I wake up to my mom screaming my name. "ZAYNAB!!!" I leap out of bed and land face flat on the floor. The bombs are getting closer. Our six-story concrete building is swinging like a tree in the wind.

We turn on the news and find out that the gunshots we heard earlier were missiles from a submarine on the other side of the airport from our home. I begin to grow familiar with the rhythm of this war. Meanwhile the internal tension and stress in my body grows in ways I avoid feeling.

DAY 10

My mom's friend returns to drive me to the port so that I can be evacuated. I want out of the country. Mom says she isn't coming with me. She says if she is going to die, she will die in her home country and that Israel will not defeat her. My mom is a one-of-a-kind resilient woman, a woman of strength and dignity. She is the only woman in our 500-person community who stays at home for the duration of this war. The other handful of people who also stay are men who protect their homes and keep an eye out for the neighbourhood, in case looters come through.

What was once an overpopulated ghetto is now a deserted concrete jungle, with no clothes hanging on clotheslines or people yelling from the higher floors of the elevator-free apartment buildings, as they drop their baskets on a long rope down to get the corner store workers to sell them a pack of cigarettes, or a cola, or an ice cream, or some potatoes.

This time when my mom and her friend take me to the port, I am accepted to enter and begin my evacuation process. I squeeze my mom as tight as I can, I shed heavy tears and make her a few promises. She does the same.

Night 10: I board a Greek cruise ship with hundreds of other people with Canadian passports. We make our way to Cypress. It takes five days to get to Canada. My dad picks me up from Vancouver International Airport upon my arrival.

Suspended Between Worlds

معلقة بين العوالم

I need to be told everything is going to be okay
I need tender love—I need to be held
I need to be told everything is going to be okay

Alienated, living with my father and his family
He won't let me stay with my brother
He says he will send me back to Lebanon,
Through the Syrian border
if I leave his home

No one knows, not my brother, my dad or my friends,
Nor do they understand
That my weary heart and blown-up mind
Need tender love, need to be held

Need to be told that everything is going to be okay

Dad and his wife half-smile from behind their frowns
How did *they* end up with my mother's daughter?
Unable to consider my humanity or my mother's
They don't nurture or express kindness towards me;
Rather they mock and shame my shattered stride

I am treated like a second-class family member
My mother is abashed for staying in Lebanon
My father, more concerned about money than my wellbeing
My brother makes me pizza and gives me a job

I try to be normal,
Meet up with my old friends
Go watch the festival of lights on the waterfront

Watch beautiful explosions in the sky

But when they pop, I can't breathe, suspended in
fear—disbelief
Will the waves of war forever live inside of me?

Most people love these fireworks, but not me
I want to run and hide but I'm stuck in the crowd
Another anxiety attack makes my skin grow thick
Growing the distance between me and everyone else

I thought I'd get to relax, put down my stress
Allow the tension to release
Instead I get more wound up
Living with my dad and his wife
Who sadly lack sensitivity, kindness, and care

I need to be told everything is going to be okay
I need tender love—I need to be held
I need to be told everything is going to be okay

The war continues, I keep up with the news

Until the day comes when leaflets are dropped on our
Beirut neighbourhood,
Warning people that the bombing campaign is imminent

I call my mom, again and again, and
Days go by with no answer

Sickness riddles my spirit
My body slowly shuts down
My jaw locks shut
I can barely move or get out of bed

I start to think my mom is dead

And then the war ends
And Mom calls
She's not dead
She's not dead

I tell her I am coming home
Mom, I am coming home

أنا بحاجة أن تخبرني أن كل شيء سيكون على ما يرام
أنا بحاجة الى حب وحنان، بحاجة أن تحتضنني
أنا بحاجة أن تخبرني أن كل شيء سيكون على ما يرام

ما زلت في الخامسة عشر من عمري، على الأكثر طفلة
أعتقد أن والدتي ماتت
ما زلت في الخامسة عشر من عمري، على الأكثر طفلة
أعتقد أن والدتي ماتت

I need to be told everything is going to be okay
I need tender love—I need to be held
I need to be told everything is going to be okay

I'm still 15, a kid at most
Thinking my mother is dead

I'm still 15, a kid at most
Thinking my mother is dead

Home

البيت

LEBANON

لبنان

IF YOU'VE EVER BEEN TO LEBANON, you will know of this phenomenon. *Ladies and gentlemen, please return to your seat and fasten your seatbelt. We are nearing the terminal and will land in Beirut at 19:21.* People make their way to their seats, buckle up, open the window blinds, and watch. We begin to make out buildings, roads, as we approach our destination. Tears fill my eyes, excitement is on every person's breath. We see the runway, the wheels go down, we touch the ground. Then the applause begins, every person is thrilled to be home. It's a moment of victory, of reunion, a deep exhale. This land we call home is ancient, it is our bloodline. Coming home to our source of belonging, of identity, of culture. It is a sacred moment to each one on the plane. Especially after the war, it was a rejoicing I've never felt before. At that moment, when the wheels touched the ground. And the plane started to slow down, my jaw unlocked. It was a miracle.

I hope this tradition, of celebrating our roots in our return home, however small or large the gestures, continues with the next generations. I hope the youth realize how, despite all the hardship that comes with our corrupt countries, that they (we) are close to what makes us who we are.

لا يمنحنا المال، والمرتبة، والمادة، ما تمنحنا إياه التربة التي نحن منها.

No money, status, or material objects can give us what the soil that we are from can.

IRAQ

العراق

My body did not know how to meet you

How to say hello to my roots in desert sands

From Kuwait, through No Man's Land, into Basra, Iraq

We saw fleets of blown-up cars, the shadows of war victims

Ships half buried in dried-up riverbeds

US soldiers in tanks speed down highways

Checkpoints every few kilometres

I got to meet my father's family for the first time

My grandmother—*Bibi*

My grandfather—*Jidou*

My cousins, aunties, and uncles

A lamb slaughtered for our safe arrival

Blood covered the terrace, as we prayed, gave thanks

We walked the streets, bore witness to starved eyes

There was no colour, no spark or shine

Just beaten-down minds, hanging on to survive

And still, the aftermath of war had not begun

When will this time come?

I wondered, as I stood on my native land
Mesopotamia, the cradle of civilization
Poisoned, stolen, beaten down, robbed of
dignity and decency

All in the name of power, of money, of greed

Iraq is a beautiful place. No matter how hard they try
to beat up our countries and communities, we, made of
resilient resistance, rise.

"يحاولون دفننا، لكنهم لم يعلموا أننا بذور."
مثال مكسيكي

"They tried to bury us, they didn't know we were seeds."
—*Mexican proverb*

PALESTINE

فلسطين

WHEN I WAS 16 YEARS OLD I asked my grandmother if she was mad that her country was invaded, taken over, and occupied by the state of Israel. She was born in Haifa, Palestine, and had to leave as a child with her family during the Nakba. She said, "No."

As a 16-year-old who had just experienced war for the first time in Beirut earlier that year, I was baffled. Not only was I baffled, I was as mad at the preposterous war that I had just experienced and the continued occupation of Palestine.

Because of my deep love for this elder, my mother's mom, I let her words sink in. It took time to grasp and digest her words. Ten years of contemplation, to be exact.

My grandmother was a Christian woman. She adored Jesus Christ and learned his ways. As he was being crucified, he said, "forgive for they do not know." He met suffering with love. He taught compassion through his example. His teachings became her practice. She met suffering, her own tragedy, with love.

أن أمارس ما نقله أجدادي مهمة مستمرة، ولكن لا أريد
أن أعيش حياتي وفي قلبي كراهية. وهذا ممكن تحقيقه ولو
بصعوبة. قد إكتشفت في حياتي أنه يستحق ذلك.

*To practise what my elders have passed to me is a
continuous task, for a life with hate in the heart is not a
life I want to live. While it is hard, it is possible and in my
life I have discovered—it is worth it.*

CANADA

كندا

MY DAD IS PROUD TO BE CANADIAN, my brother too. Why do I not feel the same way? I feel starved of culture. I feel robbed of tradition. I feel the pain of my people. Why do I get to live here, why do *we* get to live here, while others are still suffering the heavy hand of oppression? Political narratives will have us believe whatever they write on our screens.

So do not forget where you're from. Remember where you are from. I feel like a visitor here, honoured to be a guest. My roots sing to me in my dreams. A lullaby of remembrance that my ancestors are in me. I am their dream come true. I am the sprouted seed they planted. I extend across ocean and land, unable to be severed from my roots.

Our motherlands were occupied. My parents came to Canada for another chance, to a land that is also occupied. The history of this place breaks my heart. Cognitive dissonance erupts when sitting in this dichotomy; of fleeing war-torn countries to live in a country founded by the genocide and erasure of Indigenous Peoples and their history.

لا أقدر أن أنسى وأمضي قدماً، كما لو أن التاريخ لم يكن له
تأثير.

*I can't and won't forget and move on, as if history is
irrelevant.*

A Quiet Revolution

An Ode to the Vipassana Meditation Technique
Taught by S.N. Goenka

ثورة هادئة

In 2013, I took my first 10-day silent meditation course. This meditation technique has enriched a multitude of facets in my life. My poetry is layered with meditation metaphors. Coming out of suffering is a practice. Coming back to our breath, to our senses, and to the present moment sounds too simple, yet this is the first step. To see things as they are is easier said than done.

Where is your attention?
Come back to the breath
Upon what lies your awareness?
Feel into your senses
How does it feel inside?
Sit down on your cushion
When you stop and close your eyes
Go inside, slow down and begin

Detach from distraction
Phone down, ringer on silent
Unplug from consumption
Better sit with an empty stomach
Let go of constant doing
Thoughts are background noise
Drop into your being
Focus on sensations

Explore thyself
Watch tension ease
Learn and understand
Patterns speak to those who listen
The mechanics of thyself
Awareness expands and contracts

Know thyself
Be gentle with yourself

My mind spins, seeks and searches
For answers to my endless questions
How will we get through this era of confusion?
How will we overcome the falsity of separation?
How will we embrace discomfort, for the sake of change?
Can we dissolve our complacent comfort?

Polarization is rampant
Judgements all around
Information is an addiction
With no solid ground to be found

People prefer to speak than to listen
Flags are waved, opinions are planted
Made-up minds cannot see what's in front of them
Deprive our ability to reach out and into each other

I am a poet, I turn words into poems
Compose questions, search for answers
Am relentless in self-inquiry
Am full of curiosity, as I reckon with reality

And my rightful place in this world

I've come out of inner confliction
For this moment of confession

أود أن أعترف
أنني مثل البقية
مخلوقة من دم وعظام
ولحم قابلة للجراح

I'd like to confess
That I'm just like the rest
I'm made of blood and bone
And vulnerable flesh

I'm made up of stories, with an ego who feeds me lies
I've got a history of shadows and sadness deep inside
One thing is for certain, I've got the will to choose

So I exercise my power
Sit down on my cushion
To close my eyes and withdraw
Come back to the breath
Get to the bottom of my suffering
Feel into my senses
Pull it by the roots
Observe, don't react

In order to do so
Watch tension ease
I've got to get to know myself
Patterns speak to those who listen
I've got to get honest
Awareness expands and contracts
See things as they are
Be gentle with yourself

There is no time for pretend
For make-believe and delusion

In order to heal, I've got to see clearly
Be gentle with yourself
How it is that I cause my own agony
Observe, don't react

I'm only 33, like you, I'm learning on my way
When I close my eyes and go inside
Come back to the breath
I come face to face with what caused me fear
Feel into my senses
From looking at the pain
Watch tension ease

Why do we become addicts of good feelings
Why do we push away the rest
There's got to be more to us
Than the narrative in our heads

The currency of vulnerability
Is a handshake with honesty
Because being real isn't pretty
It does not fit in a box
Being real grows out of broken pavement
And scribbles outside the lines

This is why I withdraw from distraction
To slow down and connect with the changing nature of
my being
So that I may continue to become
While constantly letting go

In the name of vulnerability,
I step closer to my truth
Honesty is what is needed
For my freedom and for yours

May this spark your action
Inside and out
If not now, then when
If not us, then who
Close your eyes and begin

ZAYNAB MOHAMMED

هل أنت تسمع؟

ARE YOU LISTENING?

We Are Not the Same

لسنا متشابهين

It is common, for me, to be asked where I am from. I wonder if it's because of the colour of my skin? Perhaps it is my Arabic name? Maybe it is because I don't fit into the norm where I live?

My response is to ask those who ask me where I am from where they are from in return. But really, where are you from? And how do you spell your name?

(Unless you're Indigenous to these lands, you're not from here, none of us are.)

Let's be clear, the status quo needs scrutiny from all of us.

We all have a heart, a body, a brain, and blood that rushes
through our veins
But that doesn't make us the same

We were hopefully born to a mother who loved us
And into a family with many secrets
We all follow some sort of internal compass
Have reasons to wake up, go to sleep
In the neighbourhoods we've settled into

That certainly doesn't mean we're the same

The way our feet meet the earth
The way our words travel across sky
The way our hearts tremble, pierce our presence
The way we think, how we feel and see

This is what makes us unique
The way we carry our stories
The way our ancestors are with us
The way we show up, how we love
The way we lose ourselves to a vision

This is what makes us different

لذلك عندما تسمع قصة لا تشبه قصتك
تبطأ، كن فضولياً
إكتشف المزيد، من خلال البقاء منفتحاً
إسأل أسئلة
لا تجعل الأمر عنك
لا تقارن الخطى
لا ترفض أو تحكم
على الإنسان الذي يشاركك قلبه

So when you hear a story unlike yours
Slow down, be curious
Find out more, by staying open
Ask questions

Don't make it about you
Don't compare footsteps
Don't dismiss or judge
A human who shares their heart

It is time to question our limitations
Especially when they get in the way of our evolution
Or how we treat strangers
Or how we hold onto bias

If we benefit from societal norms
A structure designed to favour some over others
A hierarchy of winners and losers
This is a paradigm we can alter

May we become a society where winning is for everybody

Are we willing to help change minds
By choosing to love in the face of suffering?
Are you willing to help change minds
By choosing to love in the face of suffering?

Are we capable of shifting this paradigm
Re-build it with strong pillars
Foundation of basics
Food, water, shelter, love?

Can we pass survival,
Become a culture who thrives?

When it sees its neighbours' wings flicker across the sky
In radiance, in colour, in full human expression

A paradigm where we *celebrate* our *differences*
Knowing that this makes us resilient

هل أنت تسمع؟

ARE YOU LISTENING?

Outro

الخاتمة

My journey began as an unfertilized egg in my mother's womb
This egg was developed in my mother while she was a fetus in
her mother's, my grandmother's, womb

I was once in my grandmother's womb
She planted her prayers in me
I too carry my granddaughter's seed
Embedded deep in my ovaries

So when I bleed, shedding my seeds
I slow down to sing to the cradle of my being
I remember to sing for the women before me
I stop and think about the children to come

أغني لنفسي، لجدتي، لأمي، لبناتي المستقبلية
أغني، " أحبك، كما أنت، بآلآمك، وجمالك، وكل ندوبك
أغني، "أسمعك، من وراء الآلآم، أسمع قلبك، أسمع دعواتك

I sing to myself, to my grandmothers, to my mother, to my future daughters.

I sing, "I love you, just as you are; your pain, your beauty, and all of your scars."

I sing, "I see you, behind the pain. I hear your heart, I hear your prayers."

"I see you, behind the pain. I hear your heart, I hear your prayers; *To love, and see and care for softly.*"

Are you listening?
Joy is waking!
Are you listening?
Joy is waking!

هل تسمع؟
الفرح يصحوا
أنا أسمع

Are you listening?
Joy is waking!
I am listening!

Afterword

by Zaynab's Mom

"إذا تم العقل نقص الكلام."
علي بن أبي طالب

"The smarter you get, the less you speak."
—Ali bin abi Talib

IN THE NAME OF GOD, the most Gracious, the most Merciful, who created man in the best of manner, and into a life of toil and hardship.

Through the journey of being close to my children and loving them so much, I enjoyed every single moment of it. They are one of the most precious gifts God has granted me. I had to adjust myself into acquiring the best of manners in order to be the honest example for them to follow. That was my most important mission of my life, with the endurance of all kinds of hardships to make a difference in the world.

Was I mature enough to walk the path of perfection? It was through mistakes I learnt to be every day wiser by learning through life struggle, taking the right choices, and falling at times. My children and I endured the choices made for any act.

It is said,

"يوماً لنا ويوم علينا."

"One day for us and one against us."

So when things happen for our benefit, no proud and no reckless reactions; when it is against us, patience is the answer because patience is stability, strength, and solidity.

One quote I like of Ali bin abi Talib, son in law of prophet Mohamed:

"لا تتخذ قراراً وأنت غاضب، ولا تقطع وعداً وأنت سعيد."
علي بن أبي طالب

"Never make a decision in anger, and never make a promise in happiness."—Ali bin abi Talib

Once Jesus said to look at children and learn as to how quick they forgive each other after fights without holding any grudges in their heart.

Anytime I need help I flee to God. Through supplications and prayers, strength occurs.

"ففروا الى الله !" القرآن الكريم

"So flee to God!"—Holy Quran

Zaynab's *Are You Listening?* is a much-appreciated effort to send the message of love, unity, and acceptance.

After all, listening has lots of benefits;

"إلزم الصمت يستنير فكرك."
علي بن أبي طالب

"If you keep quiet, your thought enlightens."
—Ali bin abi Talib

Acknowledgements

"A man who stands for nothing will fall for anything."
—Malcolm X

I acknowledge and give thanks to the power of listening. We have two ears and one mouth for a reason. In 2020, after a six-month road trip in my van to the US, I came across this quote, and it has changed my life.

In my beliefs, fear of standing out was a cloak I liked to wear. When George Floyd was murdered, I was moved, like so many, to the streets. From past experiences, I knew that standing up for racial justice came with pushback. Yet when my neighbour invited me to the protest she was organizing, I felt a deep need to attend. The region in which I live is predominantly white, and I felt that I needed to represent and stand with the few other people of colour. So I went, I spoke and I helped where I could.

This was a moment of taking a stand for something.

Since childhood, I have noticed how people tend to speak a lot more than they listen.

After that, a woman who runs an organization in my area invited me to participate in their inaugural artist residency program. The only thing I needed to provide was a question I wanted to explore, with the other three artists who had also been invited.

I knew I wanted to explore what listening is, in all the ways possible.

From here on, my life's path got clearer every step I took. I wrote a few grant proposals to get funding to research and create artwork around listening. Several attempts later, I got my first grant and started my research. That same year, I became a BC Culture Days Ambassador.

From interviewing 47 people and making a short film with soundbites from these interviews to experimenting with new ways to express myself, I began to dream. From this writing, my one-woman show came to life. The Columbia Kootenay Cultural Alliance and the Columbia Basin Trust funded me to write the first draft of my show. The Canada Council for the Arts also funded me to write and produce it.

Three years later, my show met the stage. Since then, I have performed to numerous sold-out audiences and performed *Are You Listening?* for hundreds of people.

The biggest takeaway from these years of exploration is the ability to listen to myself more and to other people less. Surprised by every step of this process, I must acknowledge the power of art and creation. It is a transformative and challenging tool, one that I am immensely thankful for, and one that has given me the strength to show up in this world as I want to show up.

Before I go telling folks my story or my findings about listening, I must first honour my findings by practicing what I preach. I've always thought that I cared about this world more than the world deserves. Through the pain and pursuit, and my relentless will to not be inhibited by the indifference our society programs within us, I listen.

About the Author

ZAYNAB MOHAMMED is an award-winning performance poet. She was born on the coast of British Columbia to immigrant parents fleeing war-torn countries. She is Iraqi, Lebanese, and Palestinian. The countries her parents grew up in, the cultures her family carries, the language of her grandmothers, the smell of tea, and the taste of sweets are what root Zaynab in her being. She pays homage to her ancestors as she weaves stories and poems to share with the world. Inspired by her family's hardships, Zaynab is a visionary creative who has been healing herself through the written word by sharing her story and by giving her audience reflections into love and empowerment. *Are You Listening?* is adapted from a one-woman show of the same title, which has been touring since 2023. Zaynab currently lives and works in Nelson, BC, where she hosts the Nelson Poetry Slam and writes custom poems for passersby.